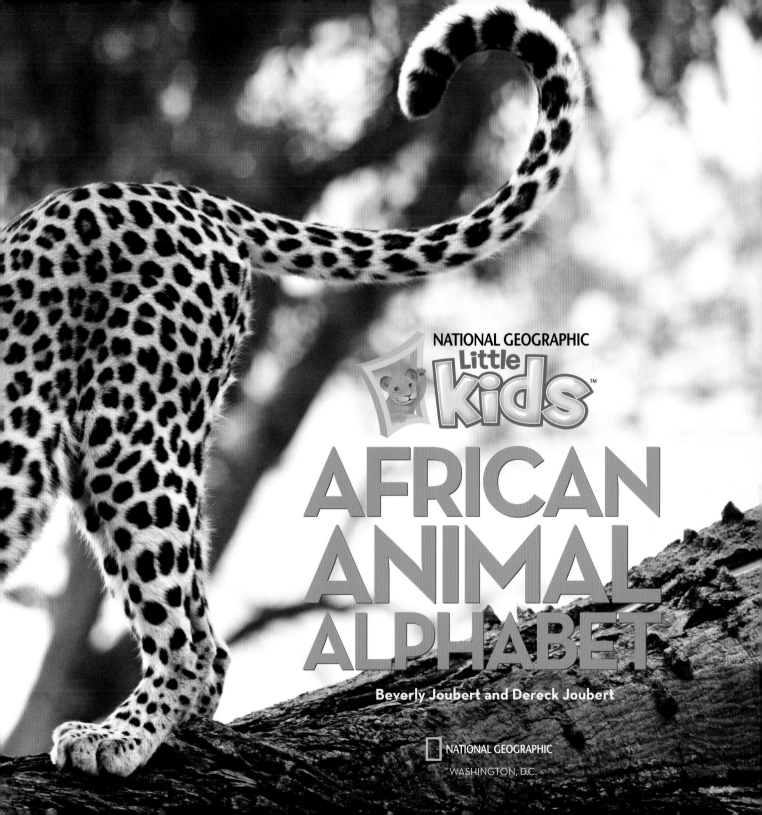

NATIONAL GEOGRAPHIC
Little
kids™

AFRICAN
ANIMAL
ALPHABET

Beverly Joubert and Dereck Joubert

NATIONAL GEOGRAPHIC

WASHINGTON, D.C.

Atlantic Ocean

A F R I C A

Indian Ocean

Map Key

  Desert

Grassland

Lake

Mountain

Rain forest

River

  Wetland

■ Jouberts' base camps

Selinda □
Duba ■□ Mombo

BOTSWANA

INTRODUCTION

As we lie in our tent at night in the African bush listening to the barks, chirps, twitters, and roars of the animals around us, we understand that all these animals have their own way of talking. We've filmed and photographed these creatures for many years and have come to know them very well. Each animal is different, just like you and me. There are giant ones and teeny tiny ones, tall and short ones, and they are always playing games. Games help the little animals learn how to be big animals, just like games help you learn what you need to know when you grow big. So here is a game you can play. As you read about the wildlife in our world, notice the letter the animal names start with, and see if you can count how many times we have used that letter on the page. For example, how many "O" words can you find on the ostrich page?

READY? Let's go on an African alphabet safari!

The adventurous Dereck and Beverly Joubert sit atop their jeep in front of two resting lionesses in Botswana. The Jouberts have spent more than 25 years living among the wild animals of Africa, learning all about how the creatures live, play, eat, and take care of each other, and sharing what they know with the world.

A is for Antelope

Antelopes are mainly found in Africa. Antelopes amble about in herds. Sometimes an antelope like this bushbuck feels adventurous and roams all alone.

Did you know?
There are 72 different kinds of antelopes in Africa.

B is for Baboon

These boisterous baby baboons are bouncy little apes that like to babble and bicker while standing on an African baobab tree.

Did you know?
An adult male baboon's teeth are longer than a lion's.

Did you know? Cheetahs are the fastest animals in Africa. They run at speeds of up to 60-70 miles (97-113 kilometers) an hour.

C is for Cheetah

Cheetahs love to chase their prey. They are calm and clever hunters. When it is time to catch their dinner, they run and pounce, then chomp and chew with delight.

D

is for Dung beetle

Two dung beetles roll dirty dung into a decorative ball as they diligently build their home using their delicate little legs.

Did you know? Dung beetles fertilize grasslands by spreading around animal droppings.

Did you know? Elephants weigh up to 14,000 pounds (6,300 kilograms) and have more than 40,000 muscles in their trunks.

E is for Elephant

A mother elephant and her elegant herd watch an energetic calf as he eagerly tries to stay just out of reach of his mom's elongated trunk.

F is for Fox

Feisty bat-eared foxes frolic and play when nighttime falls. These furry hunters find food underground.

Did you know? Bat-eared foxes only eat insects. They especially like termites and dung beetles.

G is for Giraffe

Gentle giraffes grow more than 15 feet (4 meters) tall. Their gigantic size helps them reach the green leaves on trees across the great grasslands.

H

is for Hippopotamus

Hippos spend hot days in cool water, which makes them happy. They have very little hair on their hefty bodies and are often hungry and ready for a huge bite.

Did you know? Hippos are too heavy to jump. They weigh 5,000 to 8,000 pounds (2,268 to 3,629 kilograms).

I is for Impala

An itsy bitsy baby impala stands up just a few minutes after it is born. Its mom intends to make sure her innocent baby is safe and sound.

Did you know? A baby impala can jump as high as 9 feet (about 3 meters) just a few days after birth.

J is for Jackal

Jolly little jackals are jovial and clever creatures. They like to joke with each other when they jostle and play.

Did you know? When baby jackals grow up, they stay close to home to help feed the next batch of babies.

K is for Kudu

It is hard to miss this kudu's large corkscrew horns sitting on top of its head. Kudus are king of the antelopes, but they are hard to find because they have a knack for keeping out of sight.

L is for Lion

Look! A young lion tries to climb a large tree. She hangs from a long limb, but the little lady does not look very happy to be lingering there.

Did you know? Lions eat more than 30 pounds (14 kilograms) of meat a day.

M

is for Meerkat

Mini meerkats are mindful and curious little creatures. They like to meet and mingle and play. When nighttime comes, they sleep mighty close together to stay cozy and warm.

Did you know? Meerkats love to eat scorpions. They are immune to the scorpion's poisonous venom.

N

is for Nile crocodile

A Nile crocodile shows his numerous teeth as he sticks his nose out of the water. Nile crocodiles are experts at navigating underwater and nabbing their prey.

Did you know? When their babies hatch, Nile crocodiles gently carry the newborns to the water in their mouths.

O is for Ostrich

An observant ostrich wades and splashes through the open water as it stares out curiously with its oval eyes.

Did **you** know?

An ostrich's eye is 2 inches (5 centimeters) across. It has the largest eyes of any land animal.

P is for Porcupine

A prickly little porcupine keeps its nose pointed close to the ground as it pokes and prods at the pale-colored sand beneath its paws.

Q is for Quelea

Six cute queleas sit quietly on a tree branch. These quirky creatures can fly very quickly, and they like to gather together and quibble in their flock.

31

R

is for
Rhinoceros

A rambunctious baby rhino readies his escape as he tries to roam away from his regal mother.

33

S is for Squirrel

See the silly squirrels stacked in a tree? They snuggle for warmth on shivery cold days.

Did you know? Squirrels use their front feet to hold on to food when they eat.

T is for Tsessebe

Two tiny tsessebes stay close to their towering mom. When they grow tall and strong, the time will come for them to take off on their own.

Did you know?

Tsessebes are the fastest antelopes in Africa. They can run at speeds of more than 50 miles (80 kilometers) an hour.

U

is for Umbrette

A brown umbrette walks slowly through blades of grass. This unusual bird looks unlike any other. It can use its unique beak to grab something yummy to eat under the shallow water.

Did you know?

Umbrettes are known for building giant nests in the treetops. Some nests reach up to eight feet (2 meters) in size.

V

is for Vervet monkey

Did you know?
Vervet monkeys use sounds and signs to communicate with each other.

A velvety soft baby vervet monkey clings very closely to its mother high in a tree. Vervet monkeys are vocal creatures with vociferous voices.

W is for Warthog

Baby warthogs wiggle and roll in wallows of mud whenever they can. This little warthog wobbles out to whisper little grunts to its waiting mom.

39

X

is for Xenopus bullfrog

Xenopus bullfrogs like to sit in water that is extra shallow. If you could x-ray them, you would see that they have extremely sharp teeth.

Y

is for
Yellow-billed hornbill

A yellow-billed hornbill stands perched on a termite mound with its yellow beak glowing in the sun. Does it yap, yell, or yip? No, it makes a clucking sound.

Did you know? Every zebra has a unique stripe pattern, just like our fingerprints.

Z is for Zebra

These zebras are enjoying some playtime on the savanna. Zebras have stripes that zig and zag across their bodies and create zany patterns.

ANIMAL FACTS

A ANTELOPE
HOME: forests, grasslands
SIZE: about as tall as a deer
FOOD: herbs, leaves, twigs, and flowers
SOUNDS: hoarse bark
BABIES: one at a time

B BABOON
HOME: forests, grasslands
SIZE: weighs about as much as a medium-sized dog
FOOD: grass, berries, insects, fish, and small antelope
SOUNDS: bark, grunt, chatter, and other noises
BABIES: one at a time

C CHEETAH
HOME: grasslands
SIZE: about as tall as a large dog
FOOD: gazelles, impalas, hares, and other animals
SOUNDS: chirp, twitter, hiss, purr
BABIES: two to five at a time

D DUNG BEETLE
HOME: deserts, forests, grasslands
SIZE: about the size of a thumbnail
FOOD: dung, or waste, from other animals; sometimes mushrooms and fruit
SOUNDS: chirp
BABIES: females lay 3 to 20 eggs

E ELEPHANT
HOME: grasslands, deserts
SIZE: weighs about as much as three or four cars
FOOD: leaves, roots, bark, grasses, and fruit
SOUNDS: trumpet, rumble, roar
BABIES: usually one at a time; sometimes two

F FOX
HOME: grasslands
SIZE: about the size of a large cat
FOOD: insects and small rodents or bird eggs
SOUNDS: whistle
BABIES: two to six at a time

G GIRAFFE
HOME: grasslands
SIZE: about as tall as three men standing on each other's shoulders
FOOD: leaves
SOUNDS: hiss, bellow, whistle, grunt, snort, bleat
BABIES: usually one at a time; sometimes two

H HIPPOPOTAMUS
HOME: ponds, lakes, rivers, and grasslands
SIZE: weighs about as much as one car
FOOD: grasses
SOUNDS: grunts, bellows
BABIES: usually one at a time; sometimes two

I IMPALA
HOME: grasslands
SIZE: about as tall as a deer
FOOD: grass, seeds, and leaves
SOUNDS: grunt, snort, roar
BABIES: one at a time

J JACKAL
HOME: grasslands, deserts
SIZE: about as tall as a medium-sized dog
FOOD: insects, rodents, hares, and small antelope
SOUNDS: growl, howl, chatter, yap, yelp, and whine
BABIES: one to seven at a time

K KUDU
HOME: forests, grasslands
SIZE: about as tall as a small horse
FOOD: grasses, leaves, herbs, twigs, and fruit
SOUNDS: bark, grunt, whine, smack
BABIES: one at a time

L LION
HOME: grasslands
SIZE: weighs about as much as one or two men
FOOD: gazelles, zebras, hares, and other animals
SOUNDS: roar, purr, snarl, hiss
BABIES: three to five at a time

M MEERKAT
HOME: deserts
SIZE: about the size of an opossum
FOOD: insects, other small animals, eggs, roots, fruits
SOUNDS: peep, twitter, bark, and other noises
BABIES: two to five at a time

N

NILE CROCODILE
HOME: rivers and lakes in grasslands or forests
SIZE: weighs about as much as three men
FOOD: fish and small mammals
SOUNDS: roar, growl, grunt, purr, hiss
BABIES: females lay 20 to 60 eggs

R

RHINOCEROS
HOME: grasslands, forests, deserts
SIZE: about as tall as a man
FOOD: twigs, shrubs, grass, and small trees
SOUNDS: pant, squeal, roar
BABIES: one at a time

U

UMBRETTE
HOME: forests, grasslands
SIZE: about the size of a raven
FOOD: frogs, fish, shrimp, insects, and small rodents
SOUNDS: cackle, high-pitched shrill call
BABIES: females lay three to seven eggs

X

XENOPUS BULLFROG
HOME: lakes, rivers, and swamps in grasslands
SIZE: about the length of an avocado
FOOD: insects, worms, and shrimp
SOUNDS: trill, rap, tick
BABIES: females lay hundreds of eggs

O

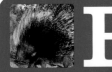

OSTRICH
HOME: deserts
SIZE: a little taller than a man
FOOD: seeds, grass, fruit, and flowers
SOUNDS: grunt, boom, scream
BABIES: females lay 15 to 60 eggs

S

SQUIRREL
HOME: forests
SIZE: about as long as a man's foot
FOOD: fruits, seeds, insects, and eggs
SOUNDS: squeak, chatter, trill
BABIES: one to five at a time

V

VERVET MONKEY
HOME: grasslands, forests
SIZE: about the size of a raccoon
FOOD: fruit, insects, eggs, seeds, and leaves
SOUNDS: woof, grunt, growl, and other noises
BABIES: one at a time

Y

YELLOW-BILLED HORNBILL
HOME: forests
SIZE: about the size of a large crow
FOOD: termites, ants, seeds, and spiders
SOUNDS: cluck call
BABIES: females lay three to four eggs

P

PORCUPINE
HOME: forests
SIZE: weighs about as much as a beaver
FOOD: bark, roots, leaves, and fruit
SOUNDS: grunt, snuffle
BABIES: one to four at a time

T

TSESSEBE
HOME: grasslands
SIZE: about as tall as a pony
FOOD: grass
SOUNDS: snort, bark
BABIES: one at a time

W

WARTHOG
HOME: grasslands
SIZE: weighs about as much as one man
FOOD: grass, roots, berries, and bark
SOUNDS: squeak, grunt, whine
BABIES: one to seven at a time

Z

ZEBRA
HOME: grasslands
SIZE: about as tall as a small horse
FOOD: mostly grass, some twigs and leaves
SOUNDS: bray, bark, soft snort
BABIES: one at a time

Q

HOME: grasslands, forests
SIZE: about the size of a sparrow
FOOD: seeds and grain
SOUNDS: chatter; mixture of harsh and melodious notes
BABIES: females lay two to four eggs

QUELEA

GLOSSARY

BICKER: to argue

BOISTEROUS: noisy and rowdy

CURIOUS: excited to learn

DELICATE: easy to damage, fragile

DESERT: a place that gets very little rain. It can be sandy, rocky, hot, or cold

ELONGATED: stretched out

FOREST: a large area of land that is covered with trees

GRASSLAND: land covered in grasses instead of shrubs and trees

LAKE: a body of water that is surrounded by land

MOUNTAIN: the highest kind of land

NAVIGATE: find your way

OBSERVANT: notices surroundings

RAIN FOREST: a wet tropical environment full of plants and animals

RAMBUNCTIOUS: wild and active

REGAL: grand and impressive

RIVER: a large stream of water that flows across the land

SAVANNA: the flat grasslands of Africa

UNIQUE: one of a kind

VENOM: a poisonous fluid that some animals produce and pass to a victim through stinging or biting

VOCIFEROUS: calls out loudly and often

WETLAND: an area that is mostly covered in shallow water, such as a swamp

MORE INFORMATION

For more information about African animals and many more, check out these books and Web sites.

BOOKS

Galvin, Laura Gates. *Alphabet of African Animals*. Norwalk, CT: Soundprints, 2008.

Haas, Robert B. *African Critters*. Washington, DC: National Geographic, 2008.

Hughes, Catherine D. *National Geographic Little Kids First Big Book of Animals*. Washington, DC: National Geographic, 2010.

Johns, Chris. *Face to Face with Cheetahs*. Washington, DC: National Geographic, 2008.

Joubert, Dereck, and Beverly Joubert. *Face to Face with Elephants*. Washington, DC: National Geographic, 2008.

Joubert, Dereck, and Beverly Joubert. *Face to Face with Leopards*. Washington, DC: National Geographic, 2009.

Joubert, Dereck, and Beverly Joubert. *Face to Face with Lions*. Washington, DC: National Geographic, 2008.

National Geographic Kids Wild Animal Atlas. Washington, DC: National Geographic, 2010.

Nichols, Michael, and Elizabeth Carney. *Face to Face with Gorillas*. Washington, DC: National Geographic, 2009.

Tuchman, Gail. *National Geographic Readers: Safari*. Washington, DC: National Geographic, 2010.

WEB SITES

African Wildlife Foundation: http://www.awf.org/section/wildlife/gallery

Defenders of Wildlife: http://www.kidsplanet.org/

National Geographic Kids: http://kids.nationalgeographic.com/kids/animals/

National Zoo: http://nationalzoo.si.edu/Animals/AfricanSavanna/afsavskids.cfm

San Diego Zoo: http://www.sandiegozoo.org/kids/

Published by the National Geographic Society

John M. Fahey, Jr., *President and Chief Executive Officer*
Gilbert M. Grosvenor, *Chairman of the Board*
Tim T. Kelly, *President, Global Media Group*
John Q. Griffin, *Executive Vice President; President, Publishing*
Nina D. Hoffman, *Executive Vice President; President,
   Book Publishing Group*
Melina Gerosa Bellows, *Chief Creative Officer, Kids and Family,
   Global Media*

Prepared by the Book Division

Nancy Laties Feresten, *Vice President, Editor in Chief, Children's Books*
Jonathan Halling, *Design Director, Children's Publishing*
Jennifer Emmett, *Executive Editor, Reference and Solo, Children's Books*
Carl Mehler, *Director of Maps*
R. Gary Colbert, *Production Director*
Jennifer A. Thornton, *Managing Editor*

Staff for This Book

Priyanka Lamichhane, *Project Editor*
Eva Absher, *Art Director*
Lori Epstein, *Illustrations Editor*
Dawn McFadin, *Designer*
Kate Olesin, *Editorial Assistant*
Carl Mehler, *Map Production*
Grace Hill, *Associate Managing Editor*
Lewis R. Bassford, *Production Manager*
Susan Borke, *Legal and Business Affairs*

Manufacturing and Quality Management

Christopher A. Liedel, *Chief Financial Officer*
Phillip L. Schlosser, *Senior Vice President*
Chris Brown, *Technical Director*
Nicole Elliott, *Manager*
Rachel Faulise, *Manager*
Robert L. Barr, *Manager*

The National Geographic Society is one of the world's largest nonprofit scientific and educational organizations. Founded in 1888 to "increase and diffuse geographic knowledge," the Society works to inspire people to care about the planet. National Geographic reflects the world through its magazines, television programs, films, music and radio, books, DVDs, maps, exhibitions, live events, school publishing programs, interactive media and merchandise. *National Geographic* magazine, the Society's official journal, published in English and 32 local-language editions, is read by more than 35 million people each month. The National Geographic Channel reaches 310 million households in 34 languages in 165 countries. National Geographic Digital Media receives more than 13 million visitors a month. National Geographic has funded more than 9,200 scientific research, conservation and exploration projects and supports an education program promoting geography literacy. For more information, visit nationalgeographic.com.

For more information, please call
1-800-NGS LINE (647-5463) or write to
the following address:

National Geographic Society
1145 17th Street N.W.
Washington, D.C. 20036-4688 U.S.A.

Visit us online at www.nationalgeographic.com/books

For librarians and teachers: www.ngchildrensbooks.org

More for kids from National Geographic: kids.nationalgeographic.com

For information about special discounts for bulk purchases, please contact National Geographic Books Special Sales: ngspecsales@ngs.org

For rights or permissions inquiries, please contact National Geographic Books Subsidiary Rights: ngbookrights@ngs.org

Hardcover ISBN: 978-1-4263-0781-2; Library ISBN: 978-1-4263-0782-9

Photo credits: All photographs by Beverly Joubert unless noted here: pp. 30-31, David Hosking/age fotostock/photolibrary.com; p. 36, Philippe Clement/naturepl.com

Image on page 1: A young mountain gorilla shows off a gigantic grin as he happily hangs from a tree.

Image on title page: A leopard stretches out on a long tree limb as its tail makes a little loop.

Printed in China

11/PPS/1

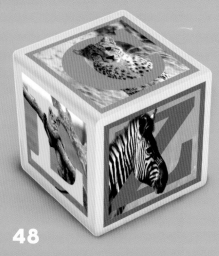